BORTHWICK INSTITUTE OF HISTO
UNIVERSITY OF YORK

The Anglican Clergy and Yorkshire Politics in the Eighteenth Century

by

Richard Hall
University College, Worcester

and

Sarah Richardson
University of Warwick

BORTHWICK PAPER No. 94

First Published 1998

ISSN: 0524–0913

ISBN 0-903857-52-9

The cover illustration is taken from a Tory pamphlet of 1709 showing the threat perceived from Low Church, Whig proposals, reproduced courtesy of the British Library.

The emblem on the front is a copy of the central boss in the roof of St Anthony's Hall and represents the pig, traditionally associated with St Anthony the Hermit.

Acknowledgements

We are grateful to the trustees of the various manuscript sources that we have utilised for their permission to reproduce material here, especially those of the Wentworth Woodhouse Estate, and the deans and chapters of Ripon and York. We would also like to thank the staff of the archives which we have used for their time and consideration; a particular mention needs to be made for the staff at the Borthwick Institute of Historical Research who have proved extremely efficient and helpful.

Thanks are also due to Professor Bill Speck for his critical comments and support.

Abbreviations

BL. Add.	British Library, Additional Manuscripts
HMC	Historical Manuscripts Commission

The Anglican Clergy and Yorkshire Politics in the Eighteenth Century

The Anglican clergy possessed formidable political power in eighteenth-century society. Marked out by their black clerical dress they were a potent symbol of electoral influence when they rode or marched to the poll at county elections as a body to cast their vote in a phalanx for their preferred candidate(s). The most notorious occasion was the 1710 election in the wake of the Sacheverell crisis when cries of 'the Church in danger' mobilised the clergy to support the Tory party against the Whig apostates. It was reported at the Yorkshire election that 'the Dean with a great body of clergy voted for Downes and Kay, the Church Party candidates'.[1] Their power and influence was routinely recognised by the candidates who traditionally directed their election addresses to the *clergy* and gentlemen of the county. The clergy, when they acted in concert, were a significant source of political power.

However, they were of greatest political import as individuals, in their role as parish priests at the centre of local society.[2] At all levels of politics – vestry, local and national – personal contacts were essential and the local incumbent was at the centre of these neighbourhood political networks. The parish priests acted as land stewards to local landowners, managed schools, administered charity and policed the neighbourhood via the ecclesiastical courts. They performed myriad social tasks for the local community which in turn provided them with immense influence. The clergy acted as a link between the gentry and the local populace; merging with and mediating between competing local elites. County electoral politics were essentially local parish politics writ large and connected together. The clergy acted as assiduous canvassers, politickers, conduits of information and electoral agents. As active citizens, although they could not put themselves forward for Parliament, they exercised their right to participate in local politics and it was incumbent upon them to use the influence they possessed to further the cause of Christianity (whatever they interpreted that to mean). Even clerics at the top of the church hierarchy would engage in canvassing for their favoured candidates. For example, the archdeacon of York, Robert Markham, wrote to the Tory candidate Henry Lascelles during campaigning for the 1806 election:

> Not a single person has canvassed for you in any place I have gone to – nor has a single paper ever been received by a freeholder from you, requesting them to give you their support... How is it possible that any friend of yours can do anything more particularly when there is no agent to whom he can apply for a list of voters. I have already tired both my horses, but I am not tired myself – let us see some more vigour or we shall both be tired – if you lose your election, it will be your own fault.[3]

Not surprisingly Lascelles aborted his candidature and the county election contest of 1806 was left uncontested. This example illustrates the unique position of clergymen and their value to the politicians as canvassers and advisors.

If roused, the Anglican clergy could be a formidable engine of political power. However, the eighteenth-century Church has been presented by a number of diverse commentators as an institution in crisis countering this picture of clerical authority.[4] The Church, it is argued, was gradually losing its social, political and religious authority throughout the century. It was tainted by corruption, suffered diminishing congregations, was threatened by the rise of nonconformism and was losing its central local social role.[5] The popular caricature of a priest was that portrayed in the satirical ballad *The Vicar of Bray* where the local parson changed his views following each transfer of political power. All of the above contain elements of truth. The advent of the Hanoverian monarchs changed the nature of the Church-State relationship which had been in constant crisis since 1688. The suspension of Convocation in 1717 removed a potential theatre of conflict.[6] Although Atterbury had failed to gain support for his High-Church plans in 1710, because of a co-operation between both High and Low-Church divines Convocation was still seen as an important factor in the running of the Anglican machinery. After 1717, as bishop Warburton of Gloucester put it, 'to have laws framed and modelled solely by the State, and (without previous communication) imposed on the Church, is making of it the meanest and most abject of all the State's creatures'.[7] Many clerics feared that the autonomy of the Church was lost and that the secular heads of state would come to dominate it. The Whig politicians also brought the system of patronage and preferment under their close political control, making it effective as a means of diffusing political discontent generated by the senior clerics.[8] The abuse of the patronage system, widespread pluralism and nepotism led to local priests losing spiritual and political authority over their congregations, who either stopped attending services altogether or transferred their allegiances to rival denominations.[9] These faults existed, and the eighteenth century can be seen as a transitionary period; but this analysis of the Church-State relationship obscures the continuing effectiveness of the local clergy in electoral politics.

This continued electoral effectiveness mirrored the expansion of party organisation undertaken in the eighteenth century. O'Gorman has shown how political management increased as the century wore on and that the patronal classes had to work extremely hard in order to gain favour with the electorate.[10] In this way electoral activity became essentially local and community based, although county elections were organised on a county-wide scale. Within Yorkshire in the first half of the eighteenth century the Whigs undertook a massive overhaul of their electoral mechanisms and moved away from the ad hoc organisation that had existed in Anne's reign. This bore fruit in and after 1727 and forced the Tories to alter their organisation also.[11] The developments made by the Whigs meant that they managed to secure at least one shire seat at the general elections of 1727 and 1734, and also won the by-elections of 1727 and 1742.

This shift towards the Whigs also occurred amongst the clergy. The support which was given to the Tories in 1708 and especially during the Sacheverell election of 1710 was lost to that party and by mid-century a majority of the Yorkshire clergy were Whigs. However, in order to explain this shift it is important to understand who these clerics were and the nature of their patronage ties. These points were taken up by Baskerville when he looked at the political role of the Cheshire clergy. He wrote that 'Without such additional data and analysis, we may know in broad outline what happened to the votes of some members of the Hanoverian clergy, but we cannot hope to explain why.'[12] This transformation in the politics of the Yorkshire clergy can also be further illustrated by looking at its allegiance and actions in the later eighteenth and early nineteenth centuries, when there was a move back towards the Tories. Although this was a different stage in the development of the politics of the clergy, it places them clearly within the shifting scene of party evolution in Yorkshire.

I

The religious ideology of the eighteenth century was crucial to the strength of the political parties. Anne's reign saw the most heated concentration of political activity, with religion as a major factor. With the accession of Queen Anne, the clergy and their supposed political vehicle, the Tory party, saw a monarch who would give the Anglican Church the support they felt it needed after the upheaval of the 1688 Revolution and the Toleration Act had severely damaged their collective psyche. The Queen stated that 'I know the principles of the Church of England and I know those of the Whigs; and it is that and no other reason which makes me think as I do of the last.'[13] The division of high politics seemed to be a dichotomy between the Tory High-Church and Whig Low-Church parties. The sub-dean of York, William Pearson, wrote to the Tory archbishop, John Sharp, that 'I should be glad to find their Parties taking any other Badge to distinguish themselves by than that nonsensical one of High-Church and Low-Church which has done us so much mischief.'[14] Although specifically referring to Scotland, Pearson's comments mirror those of the Yorkshire antiquary Ralph Thoresby, who stated that English politics and society were riven by 'the wretched distinctions betwixt High and Low Church'.[15]

This religious fracture was hardened by the Whig impeachment of the Tory divine Dr Sacheverell. This perceived attack on the very ideological fabric of the Church was the one factor that ensured the Tory landslide at the 1710 poll. Within Yorkshire this election saw the two Tory candidates garner well over 6,000 votes each whilst the only Whig who could be persuaded to stand mustered a mere 3,000.[16] However, one contemporary noted that 'Had they [the Church party or Tories] made less of an appearance of contempt the modest partys of their own church would have better liked them.' Moreover, he added, the Whig candidate Sir William Strickland, was 'a true Church of England man',[17] despite being painted as the opposite. This indicated that there were moderates among the clergy.[18]

Such moderation was an impossible dream for many clerics, for whom the notion of the 'Church in Danger' from the Whigs, was a pervasive argument. At the visitation of 1695 the archdeacon of York, Knightly Chetwood, had railed against Whig-inspired 'dissenters coming in unto the blessed Church of England'.[19] What the Tories wanted was a Church untainted by either Dissent or Catholicism; thus they could quite happily back the monarch, be it through signing the Association to William III in June 1696, or through allegiance to Anne. As long as the Church of England was untarnished in its purity they had no complaints. The Whig belief was that the Tories were a mere step away from reasserting non-resistance as a political creed and reverting to the succession of the exiled Catholic, James Stuart. The Reverend Richard Stretton wrote to Ralph Thoresby in March 1710 that 'All the Papists, priests and Jesuits in town

[London], are zealous for Dr Sacheverell.'[20] By implication the Tories and High-Church prelates were tarred with the same brush and the general election that followed in October kept the religious ill-feeling on the boil. Indeed two months after this contest Thoresby informed the Reverend John Strype about 'the present ferment, which is not allayed in these parts [the North]. A gentleman of £400 per annum was barbarously slain near Hull, for arguing the low church...'.[21]

A report from 1702 had contended that,

> at an Election in Yorkshire, in the midst of poleing, stood up a fellow who ball'd out as loud as he was able, 'I publish the banes of Matrimony between the Church of England and the Church of Rome, if any person knows a lawfull impediment, let them speak'. The loudness of the speach surprised everyone, at last stood up another who forebad the banes the reason being requir'd, because the two churches are so near a kin.[22]

This was a crude representation of the Augustan Anglican Tories as a party with crypto-Jacobite sentiments, whereas in reality the Tories and Anglicans in Yorkshire were never Jacobites. One Tory cleric, the rector of Barwick-in-Elmet, George Plaxton, supported the Church as established in law and balked at the idea of a return to Catholicism. Indeed, in 1707 he wrote to the archbishop about Sir Thomas Gascoigne, a recusant neighbour who had recently sought shelter in his church: 'Sr Tho Gascoigne calls himself a Protestant, and so do the Independents, Quakers, Presbyterians etc. but Sr Tho like them is a Protestant of an ill Edition'.[23] Beyond this Plaxton saw strong ties between Anglicanism and the Tories; he wrote 'God preserve us, for 'tis his arm only [the Tory party] that can defend his Church'.[24]

Clerics like Plaxton sought a unified, strong Church of England which would not yield to the twin vices of Recusancy and Dissent. They wanted honest, resident men to be given vacant livings; men who would provide a staunch Anglican lead in their parish. During Anne's reign these hopes were reflected among many of the clergy; for instance a Tory canvass of some townships in the North Riding in 1710 found Mr Bruce, the rector of Middleton Tyas, 'a very hearty old fellow and an utter enemy to Whiggism.' Similarly, Mr Neal, the vicar of Northallerton, would support 'any gentleman of the Church'.[25] Most important to such men was the strength of Anglicanism, and they differed from their Whig counterparts not by any spoken allegiance to the Stuart cause, although some may have desired a return of King James, but rather in their perceptions of the threat to the established order caused by the Toleration Act of 1689. They also feared the subservience of the Church to Parliament, especially the Commons who 'are commonly a company of irreligious wretches who cares nothing what they do, nor what becomes of the church and religious things, if they can but get their hawkes, hounds, and whores, and the sacred possessions of the church'.[26]

This final point was driven home for many Tories after the Hanoverian succession when they saw their church under threat from a foreign Protestant Prince and his Low-Church Whig advisers; thus they attacked the nature of preferment and ideology in Church and State. The Address at the beginning of the Convocation of 1741 summed up the public side of the Whig ecclesiastical cause; it called upon God to 'support and defend our holy Religion, as by the laws of the Realm now happily established in the Church of England'.[27] It also reiterated support for the House of Hanover. For many Tories this public face hid a more devious plan; they saw the Whig lay hierarchy and episcopacy as subverting the Church's true design by increasing toleration of Dissenters and smothering the spiritual and temporal roles of Anglicanism.

Many clerics perceived this smothering as being enabled by the increase in careerists. One pamphlet stated of the average bishop that 'the fleece is all he wants, the flock may wander where they list.' The average Cathedral Chapter talked of God 'for whose Honour they Pretend to meet', whilst a scenario was painted of the general preferment of 'friends and creatures'.[28] For those in opposition to the establishment this pointed to an attack on the faith of the public. The curate of Hunslet, present at a meeting of clergy at The Angel Inn in Leeds in the 1750s, decried the fact that 'all clergymen [met], and yet not one word of spiritual things among us'.[29] To many this was the unacceptable face of a latitudinarian Church policy.

One nominally Whig cleric, William Bowman, the vicar of Dewsbury, attacked the state of religious belief among the clergy and was suspended on a basic income for a sermon he preached at Wakefield in 1731. In his printed speech he declared that:

> Nothing then can excuse an ambitious Priesthood, who tamper with the consciences of Men, who preach up Doctrines unknown to the Scriptures, and make void the Commandment of God by their Tradition; who have more regard to their own Greatness, than the Salvation of those to whom they preach, and who prefer their authority over, not their care of, the Churches.[30]

Had Bowman not had the pamphlet printed he may have got away with his less than flattering sentiments towards the Whig hierarchy. However, a long drawn-out dispute took place and he was suspended from a living in the presentation of the Crown. In 1727 and 1742 he voted Whig, however, in 1734 he could or would not poll; his defiance of ecclesiastical authority saw him become the living representation of the irreligion that the Tories saw pervading the state. Bowman himself protested his innocence and begged forgiveness; he had no desire to become a martyr, more especially as the Whigs declared that he had offended 'the whole body of the clergy'. However, it took until 1736 for him to recover his living when he recanted in front of several clerics, both Tory and Whig .[31]

The Tories would see this persecution for the sake of conscience as typical of the godless society the Whigs were creating; that a Whig vicar in a prominent manufacturing area should agree indicates that not all clerics were time-servers or unaware of their higher duties. In 1740 Bowman's son, another Whig vicar of Dewsbury, produced a pamphlet that attacked 'The Imposture of Methodism and the nature of this new Dissent'.[32] Clearly some Whigs were cool towards toleration and the view of the Church that the episcopate held. On the other hand, some Whigs still feared the appearance of Tory divines of 'such coercive sentiments and misguided zeal, [who will not] ever think the Church out of Danger so long as their great grievance, the Toleration act, is subsisting'.[33]

There is no doubt that many clerics saw political animals struggling for control of the vehicle of their faith. That their faith was strong is not in question; Mather has written that 'English Churchmanship of the Georgian epoch was "Higher" in a spiritual sense than is commonly supposed'; similarly Ollard noted that the bulk of Yorkshire's clergy were 'conscientious and dutiful'.[34] However, these men were divided in how they thought the interests of the Church would best be served. Neither Tory nor Whig parsons were particularly enamoured of the Stuarts or a Restoration. Beyond that point, issues of time-serving and patronage, as well as faith and duty, come into play. How did the clerics act once they entered the political stage?

II

At the four Yorkshire elections that took place in the early eighteenth century the number of voters who were noted as being clergymen were as follows:[35]

TABLE 1

ELECTION	NO. OF CLERICS	NO. OF VOTERS
1708	146	9,289
1727	256	11,585
1734	422	15,351
1742	371	15,063

The increase in numbers matched the overall increase in the number voting at the elections; however, the proportion of clerics in the overall number of voters rose from 1.5 per cent in 1708 to 2.7 per cent in 1734. The excise issue and the strength of the opposition to the government made the 1734 election a heated event;[36] it is perhaps unsurprising that the by-election of 1742, with no such issue at the fore, attracted fewer clergy to the polls, although other ideological and logistical problems may have played a part in this decrease.

In all 783 different clerics polled during these elections; 468 voted once, whilst 315 polled two or more times. This suggests a high turn-over of clerical voters, although many of those who polled only once could have polled twice had they so desired, since they held their benefices across more than one poll. Of those who only voted once, 181 were Tories or Opposition party voters, 242 Whigs or Government party voters, 42 gave cross-party votes and three gave votes for the independent Whig in 1708. Of those voting more than once 181 were consistent Whig or Government voters, 70 were Tories or Opposition men, whereas 64 switched sides. Thus there was a high level of party activity, alongside a differentiated religious and political ideology, among the clergy.

Of the 783 clerics, the bulk were perpetual curates, rectors or vicars. Only 66 were stipendiary curates; perpetual curates numbered 155, with 203 rectors and 273 vicars. Fourteen were schoolmasters and seven held prebendal stalls or were doctors of divinity who did not appear to poll for their benefice. Of the other 65 men noted as clerics in the pollbooks, three were, in fact, Quakers and three Presbyterians,[37] whilst ten were mere deacons not yet ordained priest. Forty-eight clerics could not be found by utilising the Visitation and Institution Act Books; whilst these men remain enigmatic they ought not affect the overall study of the clergy as a group and conclusions can still be drawn about the role of patronage and independence. However, that clearly demarcated records are available for the study of the clergy, who are in this way a privileged group, and still 48 of them remain elusive underlines the difficulty of identifying individuals.

Most of the clergy were identified as Oxbridge graduates.[38] It was virtually impossible to become a clergyman in the Church of England without having attended either Oxford or Cambridge. Of those who polled between 1708-42, Cambridge provided 481 Yorkshire clerics to Oxford's 84. St John's College Cambridge was well represented with 178 men, whilst another 118 were from Trinity and Christ's, Cambridge. Most of the men were well-educated or at least noted as 'literate' (thus they could read and write Latin), with only 55 not described as literate where they were identified in the diocesan records, and only fifty-seven whose education could not be established. That so many men went to Oxbridge at around the same time did not appear to lend itself to any wider generational or environmental split in terms of politics.

A report from *The Leeds Mercury* of 20 April 1736 informed 'The Gentlemen educated at St John's College in Cambridge', that 'the Anniversary York Meeting on 6 May, to celebrate the Memory of their Founders, will be this year held at the Black-Swan in Wakefield...'. Moreover, it was hoped that this meeting would 'maintain and strengthen their good Institution.'[39] However, any loyalty towards their *alma mater* did not necessarily instil political unanimity; of the 178 clerics from St John's Cambridge, 100 were Whigs, but a large percentage gave split or Opposition votes. Lord Malton presented seven men between 1708 and 1742, of these four were from his Cambridge college, St John's, and two from Christ's. These men naturally followed Malton's party lead, but it is not possible to talk of many colleges as breeding grounds for a particular political party from these election results. Trinity, Cambridge was an exception, for of its 63 graduates who moved into a Yorkshire living, 51 were Whigs and only seven Tories. Similarly, from the Presbyterian University at Edinburgh came twelve Whigs and two Tories. Most colleges, however, followed the pattern highlighted at Brasenose, Oxford from where there were seven Whigs, five Tories and five non-party voters. Overall the clerics were well-educated men, but their colleges, whilst having slight majorities of Whigs, still provided graduates who were not institutionalised political cannon fodder.

The bulk of the clerics lived in the benefice they voted for; only 199 did not. Of these, 43 were pluralists who lived in a different parsonage from that for which they voted; a further 102 lived near to their benefice, within the parish that a chapelry fell into, or in a nearby township; only 28 were outvoters. Although 31 men lived in York or in large towns like Beverley and Leeds, only six lived above ten miles from their benefice; from these figures it may be possible to argue a strong case for local clerical influence. A minimum of 227 of the clerics were pluralists, and the bulk of these men held other livings of their own patron or similarly politically inclined patrons. For example, Trinity College Cambridge added Whitchurch vicarage to their living of Kellington where Daniel Hopkins already ministered.

The 1708 poll produced 74 Tory clerics, 49 of whom gave double votes; 26 gave Whig votes and eleven of these were doubles; 42 voters split their votes, with sixteen favouring the two most prominent candidates, the standing Whig M.P. Sir William Strickland and the Tory Viscount Downe, whilst twenty cast votes for Downe and the independent Whig, Thomas

Watson Wentworth. In terms of votes cast the Tories were on stronger ground at this time among the clergy. However, there were well over 400 livings in Yorkshire, thus the turnout of 146 was relatively low; also the number of overt Tory voters was too low to support any claim that they were a bedrock of the Tory party at the polls. Their ideological influence may have been wider, but without a pollbook for the contentious election of 1710, any analysis of the role of the Augustan clergy has to be based on the 1708 poll. In terms of clerical turnout in Yorkshire in 1708 there is little statistical evidence to give credence to the belief that the Tories dominated the clergy; many voters clearly abstained, for whatever reason.

Of the 146 voters, fifteen were nominees of the Tory archbishop, John Sharp, and thirteen of these gave one of their votes to Lord Downe whilst six polled for Downe and Strickland; surprisingly only one gave a double Tory vote. A further nineteen were promoted by the Crown or government, and whilst sixteen of them cast a vote for Downe, ten gave Tory doubles. There were 71 clerics with lay patrons and here the nature of patronage did not paint a strong party picture. Twenty of the patrons were Tories with sixteen nominees casting one vote for Downe, and only ten voting for the Tory partnership of Downe and Kaye. Of the fifteen clerics with Whig patrons, only six gave Whig votes. Amongst the other 36 clerics whose patrons were undecided as to their loyalty, or whose loyalties are unknown, the picture is again one of strong support for the leading Tory, Downe, and no strong party case. Overall the position of patrons and clergy was as follows:

TABLE 2

PATRON SUPPORT	TORY CLERICS	WHIG CLERICS	SPLIT SUPPORT	VOTED DOWNE
Split	6	3	1	8
Independent	1	0	0	0
Tory	36	6	23	55
Whig	5	7	6	10
Unknown	15	7	16	25

This indicates the lack of strength of party politics at this time, for although Downe gained a substantial number of votes from the clergy, the other Tory candidate, Sir Arthur Kaye, fared relatively poorly. The number of split votes or singles among the clerics with Tory patrons gives little indication of a strong party cause; it also mirrors the diverse nature of voting in the wider political sphere, where the number of singles was high and where party voting was not as strong as it was to be later in the century.[40] The Tories received 74 votes from the 146 clerics, but only forty-nine of these were doubles. Admittedly those who polled for the Whigs formed less than a fifth of the clerical voters, and fewer than half of these gave doubles, but this also indicates the paucity of party campaigning at this time. That 55 men voted in almost equal numbers for Downe alone, or with the Junto Whig, Strickland, or the independent Whig, Watson Wentworth, does not suggest a rigid Tory party hold over the electoral conscience of the clergy.

Only 26 of these clerics returned to poll again, despite the fact that several held their benefices throughout this period. The apparent lack of enthusiasm may have been an individual matter or may have been settled at a higher level. For example, the by-election of 1727 was not carried through to the end and many Tory clerics may not have made it to York; similarly, many patrons may have decided not to subsidise a trip to the poll. Without surviving records it is impossible to identify individual reasoning for an abstention. Henry Plumpton, the perpetual curate of Snaith in the West Riding voted Tory at all four polls; his patrons were the prominent Tory landowners, the Yarburgh family. At Levisham, in the North Riding, Isaac Wykes had been rector since 1698 on the presentation of the Etherington family who were nominally Whig; however, Wykes did not vote until 1727 when he had also become vicar of Ebberstone and Kirby Grindalyth on the presentation of the ardent Whig dean of York, Richard Osbaldeston. Clearly, the nature of a return to vote or the ability to turn out at all could depend heavily on the political enthusiasm of the patron.

Patrons would tend to look for like-minded men, or men who had won their favour, thus it would be unusual, though not unknown, to be deliberately crossed by one's nominee. Indeed by the 1727 by-election the convergence of party feeling among patrons and their charges was increasing. As party organisation improved, the number of clerics turning out and their solidarity with the cause increased. In 1727 there was an increase of 110 clerics, to 256, who polled; given that the poll was cut short more may have desired to vote. At this election the Whigs mobilised considerably more support than the Tories, gaining 173 votes as opposed to a tally of 83 for their opponents. Of these 256 voters, only 89 did not poll at any other time, due to the fact that political organisation was improving and that there was less time to wait to the next poll. Moreover, there was a turnover of place as well as patron from the 1708 election, for of the 146 places whose clerics polled at the earlier contest, 37 were not represented by a clergyman again; of these men, 30 had been Tories. This fact, alongside the increased numbers at the polls, meant that in 1727 there was a deficit of Tories from the numbers indicated by the1708 poll.

Of the 256 voting clerics in 1727, patrons have been identified for 240 of them, whilst a further eleven were priests or deacons with no benefice and two were outvoters. A further four men noted as 'cl' in the pollbooks were nonconformists; two were Presbyterians and two Quakers. For those whose patrons were found the overall position was as follows:

TABLE 3

PATRON SUPPORT	TORY CLERICS	WHIG CLERICS
Tory	41	15
Whig	16	107
Unknown	19	42

The strength of the Whigs was evident among the clergy at this poll and as Gertrude Savile put it, 'The malcontent clergy who were so in the late reign, now preach obedience, loyalty and unity'.[41] In 1727 the major increase in clerical voters came from those men with clerical patrons, be they holders of perpetual livings, members of the dean and chapter at York, or other bishops. Vicars, rectors and perpetual curates were patrons of 31 of those who voted, the dean and chapter a further seventeen and other bishops and chapters eight. It was here that the number of Whig votes increased substantially; the 26 clerical patrons who were Whigs themselves, provided a further 22 votes through their assistants; the 18 Tories provided 13 more votes for their party. With there being only two candidates, the possibility for party voting increased. Of the lay patrons, 65 out of 96 can be identified as Whig or Tory, and 60 of their nominees cast party votes akin to their own. Crown and archiepiscopal appointees were a different matter, especially if their patron had changed. For example, of the 24 voting clerics with such patrons, fifteen had been appointed by the Tory archbishops Sharp and Dawes; the change to a Whig, Lancelot Blackburn, at Bishopthorpe Palace in 1724 may have made some of these men re-evaluate their position, for only six of them voted for Sir John Lister Kaye, the Tory candidate.

This poll was a watershed in the improvement of party organisation at Yorkshire elections, a fact reflected in the correlation between patron and nominee voting as 83 per cent of clerics with partisan patrons voted in step with those patrons. That 31 men did not is perhaps more surprising; of these, sixteen had been nominated by Queen Anne and the previous Tory archbishops or their chapters. However, the fact that the Whig candidate, Cholmley Turner, was widely regarded as an independent and not a government Whig may have persuaded some Tory appointees to poll for him. Joshua Goodall, vicar of Hunsingore, nominated by the Tory Sir Henry Goodricke, ignored the latter and cast his vote for Turner, as did the perpetual curate of Rawcliffe, Charles Hall, who defied Thomas Yarburgh to poll for the Whig, despite giving a double for the Tories in 1708. It was possible to go against a patron's wishes, and the strength of an individual's will, local township interests and perceptions of the candidates and parties may have been held as more important in deciding a voting intention.

In 1734, whilst an extra 4,000 voters turned out, the clerical vote increased by 65 per cent to 422. The final tallies gave the Government 256 clerical votes to the Opposition's 137, with 29 split. At this poll the clergy-patron link was as follows:

TABLE 4

PATRON SUPPORT	OPPOSITION CLERICS	GOVERNMENT CLERICS	SPLIT SUPPORT
Split	10	13	1
Opposition	57	15	6
Government	27	185	9
Unknown	34	34	12

Primarily the increase in numbers and the consistency of party following comes from those appointed by other clerics and laymen. For example, of 65 clerics who had secular Whig patrons, 57 supported their patron. By this time the effects of twenty years of Whig government appointments and ten years of a Whig archbishop were creating a block of Whig followers. It is no surprise that 69 out of 93 Crown and archiepiscopal appointees were Whigs. The number of clerics following their patron's party-lead rose slightly in 1734 to 85 per cent. Of the 42 who disagreed with their patron 21 were clerical nominees and thirteen Crown men; that only four were lay appointees indicates the strength of co-operation and perhaps the convergence of views between lay-nominees and their superiors.

At this poll 125, or 30 per cent, were polling for the only time, a fact which reflected the energy of electioneering and the strength of feeling involved in the excise issue. These men were almost evenly split between the Government and Opposition, but it was the ability of the former to rally 174 men who had voted before, or who would vote again, that won them overall clerical support. The Opposition following was mainly from men who would only vote at this election; a mere 65 of their supporters had voted before or would do so again.

There were six men who had polled in 1727, who would return to poll in 1742, but who did not vote in 1734; five were Whigs in 1727, and all but one Whigs in 1742. Four of their patrons were laymen, with three being Whig and one with an unknown preference; the other two patrons were the Crown, and the archbishop and chapter. Quite why these men did not poll is unsure. They may have been ill or too far away to poll in 1734; alternatively they may have felt too strongly against the excise and the Government, but not in favour of the Opposition, and therefore would not poll. They may have reflected a portion of the electorate who had no stomach to support either their natural favourites, the Government party, or the Opposition whom they could not favour. However, compared to those men who only voted at this election, such principled abstentions were in a small minority.

At the 1742 election the Whigs increased their hold on the clerical vote, and once again they enjoyed huge success among those clerics appointed by other clergy or laymen. Half of the secular patrons were Whig, some 64 out of 131, and all bar three of their nominees polled Whig; of the 23 Tory lay patrons, 22 secured a loyal clerical vote. The archbishop's appointees and those of the Crown provided another seventy-two Whigs out of 86 such voters. Among other clerical patrons 70 out of 112 were Whigs and 56 of their nominees polled the same way. The overall position was as follows:

TABLE 5

PATRON SUPPORT	TORY CLERICS	WHIG CLERICS
Tory	47	16
Whig	27	189
Unknown	26	42

Of the 43 men who voted out of step with their patron's views, 27 were clerical appointees and 11 those of the Crown. That men whose livings had been granted by Queen Anne or archbishop Dawes should now vote Whig is not that unusual if they were deferential towards their new patron's Whig views.

The most unusual occurrence was that the perpetual curates of Crosstone, Illingworth, Ripponden and South Owram in Halifax parish, which were four of the eleven chapelries in the gift of the Whig vicar of Halifax, George Legh, should oppose their patron. In the first part of the century Legh's predecessor had not polled; he was politically inactive and at the elections of 1708 and 1727 only one curate voted, in each case voting Tory. In 1731 the Whig archbishop wrote to Walpole declaring a need to find an incumbent favourable to whiggism, '...on account of the very great advantage it might be to His Majesty's service in the County of York if I should live to see that vicarage filled with a proper incumbent'. He supported the presentation of a Low-Church divine, the aforementioned Dr Legh, to overcome the negative attitude of the previous vicar. He went on:

> There are in that parish 11 chapelries...in the disposal of the Vicar, all in a most disaffected corner of my diocese, fill'd with a very numerous swarm of freeholders, crowding in against us in every contest in the election of our shire knights....[42]

Legh's appointment had an immediate effect in 1734 when nine of the curates voted for the Government candidates, including the two previous Tories. However, in 1742 seven of these men returned to poll and only three supported the vicar; the coolness of the other four may have reflected the fact that the Tory candidate, George Fox, was a local man with extensive estates in the manufacturing districts of the West Riding. Moreover, Fox had also promised the freeholders of the area that he would support the improvement of the Aire-Calder navigation up to Yealand.[43] If this was the reason for the switch of votes it would show a strong correlation between local feeling or economic need and the use of the franchise.

The widely recognised rule of thumb that the Anglican clergy were generally Tory voters is emphatically countered by the experiences of the Yorkshire clergy in the first half of the eighteenth century.[44] There was a gradual decline in Tory support among the voting clerics from over 50 per cent in 1708 to just 28 per cent in 1742. This contrasts with the position in Cheshire where Tory clergymen survived in post well into the Hanoverian period and the cathedral chapter at Chester remained strongly High Church and Tory, withstanding Whig efforts to gain control.[45] It is clear that the Whig dominance of clerical patronage in Yorkshire did filter through and affect the voting behaviour of the clergymen they appointed.

Although the politically active members of the clergy achieved a high public profile, participation within the shire as a whole varied across the archdeaconries and across time. For the shire as a whole in 1733, it was believed that 'above 400 clergymen have votes in this County'.[46] It is unlikely that this figure included stipendiary curates, though it recognised the approximate number of beneficed clerics. In 1743, the three Yorkshire archdeaconries in the diocese of York, Cleveland, the East Riding and York, had a total of 520 clergymen working in them, with 113 being stipendiaries. York archdeaconry had 211 beneficed clergy and 54 stipendiaries; at the 1742 poll the turnout was 138 perpetual clerics, or 65 per cent, and twenty-one stipendiaries, or 39 per cent. Taking the same values for the total number of clerics and translating them to the 1734 election gives turnouts of 78 per cent and 18 per cent for the beneficed clergy and stipendiaries respectively.[47]

In the East Riding in 1727, there were 92 benefices, with eleven of these held in plurality; however from these parishes only 45 clerics, or 56 per cent, polled at York.[48] This poll was cut short by the Tories and this factor affects any importance we may place upon the number who voted. In 1734, the turnout of 68 beneficed clerics and one stipendiary represented 62 per cent and three per cent of the potential clerical electorate; in 1742 these proportions stood at 57 per cent, for the 60 beneficed clerics, and nine per cent, for the three stipendiaries.

Cleveland archdeaconry was the least populated of the archdeaconries in terms of clerics; in 1743 it had 88 beneficed clerics and 24 other curates. However, its turnout was larger than in the other areas, for in 1734 78 beneficed clergy polled, or 89 per cent, alongside nine stipendiaries, or 38 per cent. In 1742 the values were 67 beneficed clerics, or 76 per cent, and seven stipendiaries, or 29 per cent. The fact that the popular candidates at these polls, Sir Miles Stapylton and Cholmley Turner, were from the North Riding, probably helped increase the turnout.

From the Yorkshire deaneries of the archdeaconry of Richmond in 1708, fourteen perpetual clerics voted out of a possible total of 68, whereas none of the eleven stipendiaries polled. By 1727 the proportion of beneficed clergy had grown to 23, representing 30 per cent of the qualified clerics; there were also now four out of 21 curates who polled. After this point in time party organisation vastly improved, and although stipendiary voters showed no increase in numbers, the number of perpetual clerics who voted rose to 38 in 1734 and 43 in 1742.[49]

At the most, however, this final figure was no more than 54 per cent of the possible electorate. This perhaps indicates the difficulty in mobilising voters to journey to York from far away. It also brings into question who was to pay for these men to travel to York. Baskerville has rightly pointed out that there is no link between a living's value and the voting habits of its incumbent.[50] Indeed, although the living of Northallerton was said to be worth £300 per annum in 1726, its vicar did not poll at the next shire election although he could have afforded the cost. Similarly, Joseph Cookson of Leeds was said to have an income of near enough £400 a year, yet he only voted in 1734, despite holding the post of vicar of St John's at the time of the 1727 and 1742 polls.[51] This does, however, beg the question of how the poorer clergy managed to get to York.[52] For example, the curacy of Cundall was worth £9 in 1726, and William Peacock, the curate, augmented his income by running Wath school which carried a salary of £20.[53] However, this was still relatively low and given that he did not poll until 1742, it may well be that he had to wait until then to find someone who would stand his charges. His lay patron at Cundall was politically inactive, and his patrons at the school were five local clerics of mixed politics; it may have been a local Tory activist like the Earl of Bruce who defrayed his costs. In 1742 Viscount Irwin, who was running much of the Whig campaign in the East Riding, paid out over £35 to the rector of Boynton, Nicholas Wolfe.[54] This was probably meant to cover a wider set of costs, such as local treats, but may also have included Wolfe's costs at the poll itself. That his patron was the staunch Whig, Sir William Strickland, who one would have expected to defray his charges, makes this extra income from Irwin unusual. In general, however, the issue of who got the clergy to the polls is a difficult one to answer and a lack of active patrons in certain areas may account for low turnouts.

Overall in Yorkshire the clerical turnout would appear to have been quite low in 1708 and 1727, and at the last two polls it continued to be so for stipendiary curates; a fact made more likely in the case of these men by the cost of getting to York to poll or their lack of enfranchisement. The turnout of beneficed clerics in the three archdeaconries of York in 1734 was 314 out of 407, or 77 per cent, and of stipendiaries 31 out of 113, or 27 per cent; in 1742 the figures were 266, or around 66 per cent of perpetuals and 31, or 27 per cent of stipendiaries. There were clear distinctions between each archdeaconry; York was more populous and encompassed the West Riding where many of the clergy and political managers resided, and as such it may well have been possible for more men to be mobilised. That the turnout from Cleveland was so high is more perplexing unless ideology or local landlords were more influential in mobilisation. The major factor that appears from this analysis is the poor appearance of the clergy at the polls, apart from in 1734. A maximum of 72 per cent, and only 62 per cent in 1742, of clerics coming to poll does not indicate a high level of political enthusiasm. For example, Oliver Naylor was a non-resident rector in the East Riding, a prebend of Lincoln, and a domestic chaplain of the Earl of Carlisle, one of the most important managers in 1734. However, neither he nor his curate, George Longmire polled at either the 1734 or 1742 elections. If men such as Naylor and Longmire did not poll, it is no surprise that other clerics would not. If these numbers were so low for the clergy, a supposedly politically aware caucus of voters, it is probable that the electorate at large was much less active.

III

From these basic election results it seems clear that patrons and nominees came to see eye to eye politically as the century wore on. Certainly most patrons would have appointed like-minded men to positions that they owned. The Tory perpetual curate of Snaith, Henry Plumpton has already been mentioned as a man who was secure in the support of his Tory patron in all four polls. Similarly, Jonathan Wakefield, the rector of Sessay, was presented by the Tory M.P., Viscount Downe, and consistently polled against the Whigs. In fact, of the 70 Tory clerics who polled at more than one election, 30 were presented by Tory laymen. It could be argued that they merely voted consistently to keep their place and were time-servers; however, consistent opposition to the prevailing political tide would not gain further preferment higher up the ecclesiastical ladder, and the actions of these men does show a level of ideological consistency among some of the clergy.

Of the 181 consistent Whig voters, few appear to have voted in Anne's reign; most were appointed during the reigns of George I and George II, or were prepared to vote once it became advantageous to do so. These would probably be the best candidates for what Speck has implied were 'time-servers' in the Georgian clergy.[55] In truth this was the case for some of the clerics; for example Jonathan Bradley, appointed by the dean and chapter to the rectory of St Mary's in York, changed his voting habits from Tory in 1708 to Whig after 1727 in line with the metamorphosis of his patrons. Other clerics like the rector of Linton, James Roberts, who were appointed by non-committal patrons, in Roberts' case Robert Oates, may have had more opportunity to change their voting habits. Roberts' switch from Tory to Whig occurred over a period of nineteen years, and was a move to support a popular independent Whig.

In fact, of the 64 clerics whose voting habits in more than one election were non-party, most were appointed by non-active patrons. It was possible that ideology or a more mature outlook may have mollified some men's views. Luke Smelt, rector at Lastingham, was appointed by Queen Anne and voted Tory in 1727, however at the next two polls he cast for the

Whigs. It is not possible to tell whether he had altered his beliefs or was affected by other interests. Without diaries or letters, that sort of behaviour is difficult to assess.

It is more simple to identify men who changed voting behaviour when they moved patron and benefice. These men numbered but a handful of voters, however they do indicate a level of deference and perhaps even of corrupt views. Whilst serving as perpetual curate of Wheldrake during the 1734 election, John Teasdale gave a double vote for the Opposition; at this time his patron was Francis Annesley, a man who did not vote at any shire election in this period. However, prior to the next election he was presented with a living at Drax by the government, and accordingly he voted Whig in 1742. This may have been an ideological change for him, but it may also be an indication that ecclesiastical preferment was linked to a modification of views.

This last comment would seem to be born out by the voting habits of the 66 stipendiary curates. Of these men, 54 had patrons who voted during this period, and 51 of the curates voted in step with their patron. This may be further evidence to support the notion that it was expedient to follow a patron's lead; however, most benefactors would choose or back a like-minded man or one who had come well-recommended, to serve a cure. Even here this may lead to a difference of opinion that did not divide a partnership; when the Whig Hollis Pigot became the vicar of Doncaster, on the presentation of the mayor and aldermen, he kept the previous curate, John Holmes, and did so despite the latter's divergent voting behaviour. Holmes may well have been recognised as an able and popular cleric, whatever his political leanings. In general, however, it was only natural that most stipendiaries were politically aligned with their patrons.

Many patrons saw a great value in staking their claim to the right of presentation to a living, and in the benefits that could accrue from it. From Sussex in 1734 one of the Duke of Newcastle's managers wrote to his lord that some of the clergy were firm, but that others 'will go as enjoyn'd by their Patron'.[56] This was particularly true of the lay patrons in Yorkshire who perceived advowsons as valued property. The number of caveats issued against the installation of a priest in a benefice, until a particular named party was approached, increased after Blackburn became archbishop. At Hunslet the principal inhabitants issued a caveat after they insisted that they had the right to nominate rather than the vicar of Leeds. The fact that more caveats were noted in the Institution Act Books after 1724 may have been an administrative change; however, that nineteen caveats were issued between 1724 and 1732, and eighteen between 1733 and 1742 indicates the importance of clerical livings as property and hence political tools.[57]

This importance possibly increased the frequency with which both parties questioned the right of certain clerics to poll at shire elections. Several lists exist of questionable votes for the 1727 and 1742 shire polls, some of which include short explanations for the rejection.[58] For example, in 1727 'Thomas Gasboyn' was rejected for 'not having [his benefice] under seale'. Similarly in 1742, the vote of Robert Pearson the parish clerk of Topcliffe was cast out because he had a salary that was paid by the inhabitants and was not freehold. In fact he had voted Whig as the perpetual curate of Kilburn in 1734, and perhaps his Tory vote in 1742 gave umbrage to some of the freeholders. Other parish clerks and curates were rejected or questioned as having 'no freehold' or as a 'stipendiary substitute'. Clerics who were schoolmasters also faced problems; for example Mr Langstaff, schoolmaster at Dacre who voted for Turner in 1742 was said to teach 'for a sallary' which consisted of 'a copyhold in Knaresbrough forest' and was not freehold. Over the two elections, 19 clerical voters were rejected or queried; of these four had voted before or would do so again for the same living.

During the election petition of 1734 55 clerics had their votes queried.[59] In 52 instances the nature of landholding was the issue; in the other three it was claimed that no such person existed. This proves somewhat perplexing as only six of these men were stipendiary curates whose position could be seen as rather tenuous. One late-eighteenth-century theorist stated that 'schoolmasters and parish clerks, seised of lands by virtue of their offices, are usually admitted to vote, and curates not.'[60] With regard to perpetual curates, it was noted that their 'privilege of voting in elections...[was] by virtue of their ecclesiastical freeholds', as long as they were 'charged to some one or more of the...public taxes.'[61]

Overall there were 32 stipendiaries who polled in 1734, but the attack on clerics focused on the perpetuals and there was some confusion involved. The basis for the disputes over land and assessment is unclear, perhaps these men had not paid the relevant charges. However, of the men objected to because they were said not to exist, more evidence is available. Anthony Witton, perpetual curate of Brignall in the North Riding was objected to by the Opposition; in fact the curate's name was Wilton. Similarly, George Goundrill, rector of Atwick, was declared non-existent; however, he was very much alive and also held the perpetual curacy of Nunkeeling and the rectory of Sproatley, both in the East Riding. However, the clerics were no more a privileged body than the freeholders at large when it came to the machinations of party manoeuvring to gain extra votes.

Party strategy was the most important factor in mobilising voters, especially among the lay patrons, who were a sizeable number in Yorkshire.

Hirschberg has calculated that in the York diocese, out of 810 livings, around 40 per cent were in the gift of the establishment – the Crown or the Church. Of the rest, 42 per cent were presented by private sources, five per cent by Oxbridge colleges and thirteen per cent 'other' patrons.[62] Of perpetual curacies the Crown presented to 17 per cent, the clergy to 36 per cent, laity to 43 per cent and colleges to three per cent.

However, it is more useful to look at the nature of patronage at a lower level. Among the laity who nominated clerics in the early part of the century most were nobles or upper gentry, be they baronets, esquires or self-styled 'gentleman'. Certain men nominated to several cures, for instance Lord Malton appointed seven men. Similarly, the Whig Earl of Holderness nominated six and the Tory Marquis of Aylesbury nominated four. Other leading gentry figures such as Sir Charles Hotham presented five men and the Whig candidate, Cholmley Turner, a further five. Ten laymen also had chaplains who polled, six were Whigs and four Tories, and all these men voted as the political allegiances of their patrons dictated.[63] It is probable that more of these clerics were chaplains of the gentry, although this is difficult to ascertain from the sources.

By and large the patronage was well dispersed; 209 different individuals or groups of people dispensed the 282 lay presentations. The antiquary, Browne Willis was informed by the precentor of York, John Richardson, in 1722, that 'the Patronages have been much altered'.[64] Purchases and leases did cloud the question of clerical patronage, especially among the laity. Four were in the gift of freeholders, including the schoolmasterships of Hemsworth and Shipton, and the readership at Sedbergh. In these instances a compromise between the town and cleric may well have operated to the satisfaction of all concerned. However, of the 282 clerics with lay patrons, 169 were presented by people with a clear-cut party allegiance; 137 of these clerics gave votes in step with, and only 12 voted against, their benefactor.

Individual patrons would certainly try hard to obtain livings for friends or suitable men, even before the present incumbent had died or resigned. For example, Viscount Irwin wrote to Newcastle in support of a Mr Hitch, for the rectory of Felchurch. He stated that Hitch 'made us many friends in a Part of the county where most of the Gentlemen, I believe I may say all, are professed Jacobites'. A few months later Irwin promoted the virtues of Mr Draper to become the dean of Middleham, as opposed to Mr Place of Bedale who already 'has one of the best livings in the County and is in very good circumstances, it can be no great disappointment to him if he misses [out]'.[65] However, patronage alone was not always enough to gain a living, especially whilst the conscientious Sharp and Dawes were incumbent at Bishopthorpe. In 1700, Sharp wrote to the Duke of Leeds that,

> In this particular recommendation of Mr Ferrand to Vicar of Wakefield in case Mr Lee should die, I do most earnestly beg of yor Grace not to lay yor commands upon me: for if you will give me leave to speak my sense freely, I do much doubt whether he have all the Qualifications necessary for the discharge of so great and difficult a post.[66]

Clearly some livings were too important to give to the highest bidder.

The clerical patronage of those who polled can be broken down in terms of the Church hierarchy; one group encompasses the archbishop, and dean and chapter of York and other sees; the other, those curates that were appointed by individual parish clerics. Three archbishops were in place between 1708 and 1742 and their political and spiritual outlooks varied. John Sharp was archbishop from 1691 to 1714 and although noted as 'exceeding strict, religious and pious', he was also 'humble, affable and kind'.[67] Sharp was Queen Anne's closest clerical confidant and had been one of her chaplains. A High-Church man, he promoted the spiritual views of the Tory party without giving it overt support at the polls, despite claims to the contrary. For example, in 1702 Lady Russell complained that he was 'guilty of some prevarication' in not coming out in support of Lord Hartington at the shire election, Sharp replied that he would 'never disserve them [Sir John Kaye and Thomas Watson Wentworth] by espousing an interest against them'.[68] However, Sharp never gave wholehearted public support or meddled in any county election. He was also one of the major mollifying forces who managed to defeat Atterbury's virulent High-Church platform at the Convocation of 1711. Sharp was a politically mild yet spiritually staunch Anglican, a man who promoted the able and committed.

As such, on his death bed, Sharp nominated his successor, the equally High-Church cleric Sir William Dawes, bishop of Chester. Dawes was regarded as the leading preacher of his day, a devout Anglican who would shore up toryism for ten years. However, this also coincided with a nadir in electoral activity in the shire, and as such his political activity and influence cannot be assessed. He was succeeded by a Whig, Lancelot Blackburn, who was archbishop from 1724-43. Blackburn was less of a spiritual leader but sat well with Whig aspirations in the county. He visited York only once, in 1726-7 during his primary visitation, and made ordinations in three summer months a year at Bishopthorpe Palace until 1733, when he no longer came into the diocese.

Unlike his predecessors, Blackburn worked with the Whig political hierarchy of Yorkshire, thus much of the patronage of the Establishment was geared up to back the Whig or Government party. In 1733, he wrote to Malton stating that 'I shall not give myself the needless trouble of sending to such of my charges as I know to be in your Lordpps dependence...', but as to the rest, 'I shall take the best care'.[69] The political role of this Whig prelate was much greater than Sharp or Dawes, and of the 61 voting clerics who were appointed by the archbishops, Blackburn nominated 34. Of these men 29 were Whig voters; this is a much higher ratio of convergence than for Sharp's and Dawes' appointees. However, Sharp lived through a period of weaker party control and was himself not a political activist, and Dawes was not alive during any contests. Also, as the hierarchy altered its political colours, many lower clergy changed their voting habits out of ideological reasoning or because they had no wish to go against the prevailing tide of whiggism.

The other major source of hierarchical control was provided by the dean and chapter. As early as 1709 the earl of Nottingham complained to Sharp that the chapter at Lincoln nominated to livings by lot and were busy making 'merchandize of the souls of men'.[70] The chapter at York was not seen in this light but it did control many livings, and 58 men voted under its patronage. However, this set of clerics were not in themselves particularly active at elections, moreover the dean and chapter did not always see eye to eye. The dean was a Crown appointee whilst the prebends were appointed by the archbishop, and this could lead to problems. Whilst both Crown and archbishop had a unified outlook harmony remained; however, after Blackburn succeeded to York and appointed more Whig prebends, the Tory dean, Edward Finch, became more obstreperous. He clashed with the residentiary canons over the use of the common seal and over bell-ringing. In comparison with this it was noted that upon the appointment of the Whig Richard Osbaldeston as dean, 'in most matters he was rarely opposed'.[71] Osbaldeston was a major landowner in the East Riding and rector in four parishes. He was tutor and chaplain to George I, II and III and was to become bishop of Carlisle. As a constant supporter of the government he was joined by more Whigs in the chapter as the century wore on.[72]

Within the chapter the major canons with interests in Yorkshire included the dean and sub-dean, the chancellor and precentor, three of the four archdeacons and 22 prebends. In 1708 those who voted were primarily Tory, however, only one out of 12 cast for the joint Tory candidates. The fact that seven polled for Downe and the independent Whig, Watson Wentworth, may indicate a desire not to waste a vote by plumping; they may have wished to vote for Downe but not to vote for the other Tory, Kaye, hence the other vote was 'dumped' on Wentworth. After 1728, when he became dean, Osbaldeston may well have managed to organise more of the chapter to poll, despite the fact that only four of them were resident in York at any one time. Seventeen out of 21 who polled in 1734 were Government supporters and sixteen out of seventeen in 1742. Only two men voted Tory or Opposition at the two polls; the prebend of Knaresbrough, Thomas Lamplugh, instituted in 1712, and the prebend of Strensall, Samuel Brearey, instituted in 1722. They also held livings in the diocese which the previous Tory archbishops had presented them to, and these were the freeholds which they voted for. Their ideologies were more important to them than the beliefs of the far-off Chapter who did not contribute to their election expenses and could not evict them.

The influence of the lesser clergy was akin to that of the laity. They presented 124 clerics who polled in this period and certain men had blocks of power. The influence of the vicar of Halifax has already been discussed,[73] and his eleven chapelries were matched by the eleven that the vicar of St John's in Leeds could present to. The Tory vicar, Joseph Cookson, was more active than his predecessor Bright Dixon had been; however, Cookson did not vote in 1727 and only gave a single in 1734. Of the curates in his charge, ten polled after 1727 and two did so twice. On only two occasions were Whig votes cast, and in the main these men tended to favour the Opposition. However, Cookson was not a political activist in the mould of Legh at Halifax; whether he organised the clerics in his area to poll is unknown, but the clerical turnout from his parish at each election was never more than six of the eleven curates. As with the lay patrons, the clerical patrons in general were a diffuse company.

IV

The one major facet of the politics of the clergy that has so far been overlooked in this article is the relationship of the cleric to his locale. The 'de Coverley Papers' in Addison's essays in *The Spectator* provided a view of the Church in rural areas as a place where 'the whole village meets...the whole parish-politics being discussed'. Moreover, in that particular caricature the parson 'is everyday Solliciting me for something in Behalf of one or other of my Tenants his Parishioners'.[74] Here there is a connection between the well-being and outlook of the parish and the views of its clergy and gentry. Certainly, in some cases in Yorkshire, there was such a close tie; for instance, the Tory Sir Michael Warton left £4,000 in a perpetual fund for the good repair of the Minster at Beverley.[75]

In certain instances the local population demanded the right to nominate a clergyman favourable to them. For example, in 1707 the vicar of Long Preston was under pressure to 'relinquish all pretensions to the place', whilst the parishioners looked 'for a minister of their own election'.[76]

Quite what the problem was is unsure, but at the following year's poll, the township voted in step with their Whig vicar, John Sparke. It would seem that the support of the locale could prove vital to the continued presence of a particular cleric, especially of a stipendiary curate. At Winkersley, where the dean and chapter of Ripon were the patrons, the curate 'usually subsisted by the contributions of the inhabitants'. However, in December 1740 it was reported that the hired curate 'is grown so very scandalous and they have withdrawn I believe all their subscriptions', and called for John Wilson, a vicar-choral of Ripon, to officiate.[77] The break-down of the patronage in this parish is difficult to quantify, but in such cases the local priest may have relied on the support and confidence of his parishioners, in both spiritual and political matters.

Of the 159 townships within the county which had more than one clergyman serving in them and polling in the eighteenth century, 55 per cent had inhabitants who voted in accord with their resident cleric(s).[78] Forty townships had no clear-cut voting pattern during this period, many of them large towns with competing interests, such as Doncaster and Leeds, and even Pocklington. It is difficult to see the effect that a cleric could have in a town like Sheffield with a very large population and yet with only two Anglican churches, one of which was closed between 1721 and 1740 in a dispute over presentation. Here the role of the local gentry may well have had more influence socially and politically. However, the vicar of Leeds recorded that in the Yorkshire contest of 1734, the Opposition candidate, Sir Miles Stapylton, 'had more votes of both clergy and laity in this parish than out of any one parish in the county'.[79] In other towns some men felt that the role of the local cleric was hardly a blessing. Upon sending ale to Horbury, Lord Malton noted that it was 'a bad Town, made worse by an ungrateful Curate'.[80]

Only three towns of the 159 had clerics who voted in opposition to the general pattern within the town. At Skipton in 1734 and 1742, the township was overwhelmingly Tory, but the vicar in 1734 and the curate in 1742 both voted Whig, indicating a clear-cut political schism within the town. Similarly Halifax was strongly in favour of the Tories despite all that the Whig vicar, George Legh, could do. At times there was little alteration that a resident cleric could make to the local balance of power.

Linking townships with the clergy and gentry who were noted in the shire pollbooks gave a total of 175 places which had a resident cleric and gentleman at any election.[81] In 1708 there were 30 such townships, and in 20 cases the township votes matched those of the social superiors. Of the other ten, six had split votes where the gentleman and cleric disagreed and these were mainly larger towns like Leeds, Otley and Ripon; at

Sprotbrough the Tory gentleman and Whig cleric were the only voters; in four towns the gentleman agreed with the cleric but not with the populace. In certain places a powerful lay figure could prevent a cleric from polling; for example, in 1710 the vicar of Wensley, 'pretends no interest, being all thereabouts under the D[uke] of Bolton'.[82] Bolton was a staunch Whig at this time and there is no recorded vote for the vicar at the 1708 or 1727 poll; however, at the 1734 poll, after the dukedom had passed to Bolton's Opposition-inclined son, Clayton did give a double vote for the Opposition candidates.

From the 1727 poll, 27 places fit the criteria of townships with resident clergy and gentry; of these, 21 had place and social superiors in accord, with fourteen of them Whig. Of the other six, Pontefract had the clergy and gentry united in opposition to the town, and the other five towns had no unity at the polls. Three of these were small townships, perhaps indicating the opposing pull of the resident cleric and gentleman; alternatively the freeholders may have had other local influences acting on them. The other two towns were Leeds and Pocklington; the latter had a Tory patron until 1728 in Henry Finch, dean of York, and the vicar he appointed voted Tory in 1734 and 1742. However, at these last two elections the new dean, Richard Osbaldeston gave a rival Whig bias as did the headmaster of the Grammar School, whom he had appointed.

In 1734 and 1742 the Whigs came to dominate many townships; out of 122 townships at these two polls, 58 had a Whig unity, whilst 16 were Tory and 48 had no convergence between clergy, gentry and township. Again these tended to occur in large places like Beverley where many different influences were at work, whilst a few, like Strensall, had fewer than ten voters. In general it was only large towns like Doncaster, Halifax, Ripon and Scarborough where township votes differed from the unity shown by the resident clergy and gentry. Moreover, as the eighteenth century progressed, if clerical and gentry votes were unified, many places tended to see a correlation between the voting behaviour of these men and the place where they lived. This was not surprising for small villages like Bishop Burton where the lord of the manor, Sir Thomas Gee, was a strong resident force. In other places the local gentleman owned the advowson and harmony was promoted that way; for instance, at Escrick the local Whig, Beilby Thompson, presented the Whig William Thompson to the rectory.

Even where clerics and gentry fell out socially, this did not tend to influence wider political events. For example, in the early 1730s, James, Lord Darcy, a Whig who lived in Sedbury, squabbled with William Wharton of Gilling Wood and his nominee at Gilling, William Thompson, both Whigs. Accusations were made by both sides about damage to the church fabric, obstruction of pews and locking the chancel door during the service.[83] However, at the elections of this period Gilling and Sedbury were constant in their support of the Whigs. Similarly, in 1709, upon replacing John Hall as vicar of Ainderby Steeple, William Dennison attacked his predecessor for leaving the vicarage 'very much out of repaire'.[84] However, both men and town were solidly Whig, and in these cases social discord did not weaken adherence to the cause. Socially and politically, however, although there tended to be strong links between a cleric and his flock, the level of concord could clearly fluctuate.

V

It is possible to see developments in the political role of the clergy beyond the mid-eighteenth century, and they tended to react forcefully to issues as they arose. In the 1780s, the attention of the Yorkshire clergy was captured by parliamentary reform. Christopher Wyvill, a clergyman from a leading North Riding family, formed the Yorkshire Association in 1780 to campaign for shorter parliaments and more county members. The Association won the support of a great number of Yorkshire clergymen. Two members of Wyvill's 'inner circle' were officials at York Minster: John Fountayne, the dean of York, and William Mason, a canon.[85] The preferred campaigning tactic of the Yorkshire Association was to use personal contacts and circular letters to the leading members of the ruling class in the county. The importance of the clergy in identifying and contacting the established elite was to prove crucial to the success of the movement.

However, religious questions remained central to certain election contests into the early nineteenth century. The Whig Lord Milton's campaign for moderate Catholic relief in the 1807 contest, for example, split his supporters among the Yorkshire clergy and added to the closeness of the election result. On this occasion, however, the loss of support from the Anglican clerics was more than compensated by the strong support for the Whigs from the dissenting ministers of Yorkshire – of the 40 identifiable dissenting ministers in the 1807 poll book, 29 plumped for Milton.[86] John Milnes wrote to Earl Fitzwilliam in June 1807 that 'the influence of the dissenting clergy has of late become diffusedly great, as nearly one-half of the clothing country [the West Riding] have become dissenters of one denomination or another'.[87] There was a clear danger that the Anglican clergy were in danger of being perceived as being irrelevant in public (and even religious) affairs.

At the election of 1807, the fortunes of the Tory party, among the

Anglican clergy at least, had been transformed.[88] In the 1807 election, the first for over 60 years in the county, the voting patterns among the participating clerics were as follows: 372 (70 per cent) supported the Tory candidates Lascelles and Wilberforce; 113 (21 per cent) supported the Whig, Lord Milton and 48 (9 per cent) split their votes between the two parties.[89] Moreover, the turnouts in 1807 were very high indeed. The visitation return for 1806 identifies 563 clergymen including stipendiary curates and at the subsequent election 533 clerics cast a vote, giving a turnout of over 94 per cent.[90] The explanation for the high turnout of clerics in the 1807 election may in part be attributed to the amount of money (over £200,000) spent by the three candidates on the election, as well as improvements made in party organisation.[91]

In the absence of election contests between 1742 and 1807 it is only possible to speculate on the causes of this dramatic change in political opinion amongst the clergy. However, a turning point could have been the 1784 general election. This election was the swan song for the surviving remnants of the Yorkshire Association. Wyvill abandoned support for Earl Fitzwilliam and the Whigs and championed Pitt as the only hope for achieving a measure of political reform. Although other leading members of his committee, including Fountayne, the dean of York, remained loyal to the Whigs, the majority of the clergy appear to have broken with the party never to return. Certainly the results from the wapentakes canvassed in 1784 attest to this, for the pro-reform candidates gained thirty-five promises to the Whig's nine, with a further eight clerics who would not declare.[92] After 1784 the Whig party adopted unpopular and extreme (in the clergy's eyes) measures, such as supporting the French Revolution, extending the franchise and Catholic emancipation, and this confirmed the clergy's break with that party.

The change in opinion appears to have come from the top. The lay patrons who could be identified in 1807 were split roughly equally between the two parties, and their nominees voted largely in concert with them. Thus, for example, George Dixon, the vicar of Helmsley, plumped for Lascelles as did his patron, Charles Duncombe of Duncombe Park. Fitzwilliam's nominees such as William Preston, the rector of Bulmer, all plumped for Lord Milton, the son of their patron. However, *all* the leading officials of the Anglican church in Yorkshire who participated in the election backed one or both of the two Tory candidates, Lascelles and Wilberforce. The archdeacon of York's support for Lascelles has already been documented; Fountayne's replacement as dean, George Markham, also plumped for Lascelles as did the precentor of York, the Honourable Edward Rice. The dean of Ripon, Robert Darley Waddilove, voted for

Lascelles and the dean of Middleham, Robert Boucher Nicholls, supported Lascelles and Wilberforce. As the hierarchy altered its political colours, many lower clergy changed their voting habits out of ideological reasoning or because they had no wish to go against the tide. Thus, by the beginning of the nineteenth century, the clergy had left the tempestuous disputes of the previous century behind them and articulated their opinions with one, Tory voice.

VI

To an extent the political cause was an important part of the social outlook of the Yorkshire clergy by 1742. This became more so in the later part of the century, as the high turnout of clerics in 1807 and their involvement with wider issues like parliamentary reform indicate. Langford has written that 'many parsons were faithful servants of squires. It was not necessary for the first rank of county elites to officiate in order to secure its interests'.[93] Certainly the number of Whig clerics increased and would have added to the local control which that party enjoyed in the shire. Also, the proportion of clergy that were in support of the Opposition was less than the substantial proportion of Opposition voters who turned out in the 1734 and 1742 elections. The Whig party's control of the advowsons belonging to the Crown and Anglican hierarchy, coupled to the strong association between the voting behaviour of lay patrons and their nominated clergy, ensured that party's strength at this time. Alongside this was the new whiggism of the chapter and a vigorous dean, and the pro-government stance of those elected as proctors in Convocation. This all adds grist to the theory of the clergy as time-servers.

However, the only information we have for Yorkshire under Anne suggests a low turnout in 1708 and a low number of joint Tory voters among the clergy. Those clerics who did poll were favourable towards Viscount Downe; however, even the dean and chapter, nominally Tory, did not overtly support the Tories. Speck has written that the results of the 1710 poll and the levels of Tory support among the clergy in the pollbooks meant that 'the tory party truly was the Church party in 1710'.[94] There is no pollbook for Yorkshire in 1710 and so any account of that poll rests on supposition; it is likely, however, that few Whig clerics would have made it to York to poll in the face of the Tory backlash in support of Sacheverell. It is difficult, therefore, to substantiate any suggested level of toryism or whiggism among the Augustan clergy in Yorkshire. Possibly many of those who did not poll in 1708 and 1710 were Whigs, one can not be sure. It took the development of party organisation during and after the 1727 poll to increase the numbers of voters. Moreover, by this time twelve years of Hanoverian rule had not worn away much of the fabric of Anglicanism, and thus many clergy probably became more able to live with the established view.

Those in opposition were far from wiped out after 1727; about a third of all clerical voters were antagonistic towards the Whigs in 1734 and 1742. In any case these figures mask the fact that to many men the Whig M.P., Cholmley Turner, was decent, independent and faithful, and they may have voted for him because of these qualities rather than his political allegiance. Despite the fact that many clerics came to profess loyalty to Hanover and the Whigs this does not necessarily mark them out as grasping. This terminology covers-up the wider implications of a re-alignment of clerical patronage; it also marginalises a large number of the clergy who were critical supporters of the Whigs. Whilst there was no extension of Toleration, for example a further Declaration of Indulgence or removal of the Test Act, men like William Bowman could happily be Whigs. Few, if any, of the Tories were Jacobites, and most clerics were satisfied with loyalty to Hanover. The main difference between the Whig and Tory clerics lay in the purity of Anglicanism they would allow. The gradual move away from whiggism towards the end of the century was the cleric's hostile reaction to the more extreme policies of the parliamentary Whig party and to some extent the failure of Fitzwilliam to grant political reform during the period of the Yorkshire Association. There was also a resurrection of the slogan 'the Church in danger' which although no longer politically potent raised genuine fears amongst the Anglican clergy that the Whigs would dilute the Church-State relationship with concessions to the Catholics and the Dissenters.

Therefore, in terms of the politics of the age the clergy can be seen as a microcosm of the shire. The growth of party organisation increased turnout and highlighted certain features of the electorate, such as voters who only polled once; these were factors which were mirrored in the clergy. The importance of patronage and ideology, and the survival of a section of Tory voters, indicates a healthy vitality about this section of the electorate. As political lieutenants, foot soldiers and cannon fodder the clergy played an important role in Yorkshire elections well into the eighteenth century.

Notes to Text

1 BL. Add MSS 70421 (Portland MSS) f. 321, Dyer, 24 Oct. 1710. For more details of the Sacheverell crisis see G Holmes, *The Trial of Doctor Sacheverell* (1973).

2 J C D Clark argues that 'the agency of the state which confronted the population in everyday life was not Parliament... The ubiquitous agency of the state was the Church, quartering the land not into a few hundred constituencies but into ten thousand parishes'. J C D Clark, *English Society, 1688-1832* (Cambridge, 1985), p. 277.

3 Archbishop Markham to Lascelles, 22 Oct. 1806 cited in E A Smith, 'The Yorkshire elections of 1806 and 1807: A study in electoral management', *Northern History*, III (1967), 71.

4 For example, C J Abbey and J H Overton, *The English Church in the Eighteenth century* (1896), pp. 282-98; G V Bennett, 'Conflict in the Church' in G S Holmes (ed.), *Britain after the Glorious Revolution, 1689-1714* (1969), pp. 155-76; G S Holmes, *Religion and Party in Late Stuart England* (1975); Clark, *English Society*, especially p. 278 and E P Thompson, 'Patrician society, plebeian culture', *Social History*, 7, no. 4 (1974) pp. 382-405.

5 P Corfield, *Power and the Professions in Britain, 1700-1850* (1995), p. 129.

6 Clark, *English Society*, pp. 288-9.

7 N Sykes, *From Sheldon to Secker*, (Cambridge, 1959), p. 65.

8 D R Hirschberg, 'The government and church patronage in England, 1660-1760', *Journal of British Studies*, XX (1981), pp. 107-39.

9 Thompson, 'Patrician Society', pp. 390-2.

10 F O'Gorman, *Voters, Patrons and Parties: The Unreformed Electorate of Hanoverian England, 1734-1832* (Oxford, 1989), pp. 67-105, 385-6.

11 See R Hall, 'Political Persuasion: Politicians and the Electorate in Yorkshire County Elections, 1708-42' (Unpublished Coventry University Ph.D. thesis, 1997), pp. 16-76.

12 S W Baskerville, 'The Political Behaviour of the Cheshire Clergy, 1705-52', *Northern History*, XXIII (1987), p. 75.

13 Queen Anne quoted in N Sykes, *Church and State in England in the XVIIIth Century* (Cambridge 1934), p. 36.

14 Leeds University, Brotherton Library, Pearson Papers, MS. Dep 1989/1/5, Wm Pearson to Archbishop Sharp, 5 Jan. 1709.

15 J Hunter (ed.), *The Diary and Correspondence of Ralph Thoresby*, I (1822), p. 359.

16 The final tallies were Viscount Downe 6659, Sir Arthur Kaye 6412 and Sir William Strickland 2910; see Bodleian Library, MS Willis 9, f. 159.

17 York City Archives, Hammond's Diary.

18 Holmes, *The Trial of Dr Sacheverell*, p. 240.

19 C Jackson (ed.), *The Diary of Abraham de la Pryme*, (Surtees Society, LIV 1870), p. 58.

20 Hunter, *The Diary and Correspondence of Ralph Thoresby*, I, p. 233, Rev. Richard Stretton to Ralph Thoresby, 9 Mar. 1710.

21 W A Atkinson, *Ralph Thoresby the Topographer*, II (Leeds, 1871), p. 170, Thoresby to Rev. John Strype, 6 Dec. 1710.

22 BL. Add. 27989 (Percival Papers), f.12.

23 Gloucestershire County Record Office, Lloyd-Baker-Sharp MSS., D3549 6/1/P17, George Plaxton to Archbishop Sharp, 23 May 1707.

24 E M Walker (ed.), Letters of the Reverend G.E. Plaxton, *Thoresby Society Miscellany*, XXXVII, Part 2 (Leeds, 1945), p. 85; Yorkshire Archaeological Society, Plaxton Papers, MS 1001.

25 BL. Add. 24612, f. 15, 'Canvassing notes of a Tory candidates' Agent...'.

26 Jackson, *Diary of Abraham de la Pryme*, p. 150.

27 BL. Add. 32690, f. 401, 'The Humble Address of the Archbishop, Bishops of the Province of Canterbury in Convocation Assembled', n.d. 1741.

28 Borthwick Institute, York, Bishopthorpe Papers, Archbishop Blackburn's papers, Bp. C&P III/8/1, 'The Anatomy of a Modern B---p etc.' (London, date removed.).

29 The Curate of Hunslet, quoted by R G Wilson, 'Georgian Leeds' in D Fraser (ed.), *A History of Modern Leeds* (Manchester, 1980), p. 34.

30 Bishopthorpe Papers, Archbishop Blackburn's papers, Bp. C&P III/8/2, William Bowman, 'A Sermon Preached at the Visitation Held at Wakefield, 25 Jun. 1731'.

31 *Ibid*., Bp. C&P III/8/7, Wm Bowman to Archbishop Blackburn, 8 Sep. 1731; *Ibid*., Bp. C&P III/8/16, Samuel Hayter to Dr (Robert) Taylor, 25 Jun. 1736.

32 G D Lumb (ed.), 'Extracts from the Leeds Mercury, 1737-42', *Thoresby Society Miscellany*, XXVI no. 761, 2ñ9 Sep. 1740, p. 88.

33 BL. Add. 33344, f. 86, 'An Appeal to the Reason and Conscience of all True Englishmen' (Mr Curteis to the Duke of Newcastle, 19 Nov. 1733).

34 F C Mather, 'Georgian Churchmanship Reconsidered: Some Variations in Anglican Public Worship, 1714-1830', *Journal of Ecclesiastical History*, 36 (1985), p. 282; S L Ollard and P C Walker, *Archbishop Herring's Visitation Returns*, (Yorkshire Archaeological Society Record Series, LXXI) p. xxiii.

35 The pollbook sources were: for 1708, York Minster Library, Liber Miscellenea, Cat.22, Add. MSS. 235, County Pollbook for the 1708 Election; for 1727, North Yorkshire County Record Office, Fitzwilliam (Malton) MSS., ZPB, A Bag of Pollbooks for the 1727 By-Election, microfilm 1446 (there are no call numbers for this collection); printed versions of the 1734, 1742 and 1807 pollbooks exist in several locations, notably Sheffield City Archives, Leeds City Archives and York City Library.

36 At the 1734 poll the Tory and Whig parties were transmogrified into an Opposition party (of Tories and opposition Whigs) and a Government party. See J F Quinn, 'Yorkshiremen go to the Polls: County Contests in the Early Eighteenth Century', *Northern History*, XXI (1985), p. 145

37 This paper seeks to deal with the Anglican clergy and does not argue that these nonconformists were part of 'the clergy'. Indeed, it would be hard to imagine Quakers as clergy. For an investigation of the role of nonconformist ministers and voters in eighteenth century Yorkshire politics, see Hall, Ph.D. thesis, pp. 288-91.

38 See, J Venn and J A Venn (ed.), *Alumni Cantabrigienses*, part 1, To 1751, 4 vols, (Cambridge, 1922-26); J Foster (ed.), *Alumni Oxonienses*, (1500-1714), 2 vols, (reprint, Germany, 1968); *Catalogue of Graduates of the University of Edinburgh, Faculties of Arts, Divinity and Law* (Edinburgh, 1858).

39 G D Lumb (ed.), 'Extracts from the Leeds Mercury, 1729-37', *Thoresby Society Miscellany*, XXIV no. 549, 20 April 1736, p. 103.

40 R Hall, 'The Whigs and Yorkshire Elections, 1695-1715' (Unpublished University of Leeds M. A. thesis, 1994), pp. 80-2.

41 HMC, *Savile*, Gertrude Savile to Sir George Savile, 20 Jun. 1727, p. 125.

42 Blackburn to Walpole, 2 Jan. 1731, quoted in C Collyer, 'The Yorkshire Election of 1734', *Proceedings of the Leeds Philosophical Society*, VII (1952), p. 59.

43 Fitzwilliam (Malton) MSS., Sir Rowland Winn to the Earl of Malton, 26 Sep. 1741.

44 This view is widely held as these two examples illustrate: 'the predominantly Tory parsons were the most visible and accessible representatives of the church', L Colley, *In Defiance of oligarchy: The Tory party 1714-60* (Cambridge, 1982), p. 154; 'the surviving poll books stand as evidence of how few clergymen ever voted Whig', Bennett, *'Conflict in the Church'*, p. 172.

45 Baskerville, 'Cheshire Clergy', p. 97.

46 Sheffield City Archives, Wentworth Woodhouse Muniments, WWM/I, ? to Malton,

13 Nov. 1733. We are grateful to the Director of Libraries and Information Services at Sheffield and to Olive, Countess Fitzwilliam's Wentworth Settlement Trustees for permission to use these papers.

47 There was no Visitation return for 1733-4, the closest are for 1726 or 1743; both are equally as likely to give variations when compared directly to the 1734 pollbook, and as a rough guide to turnout either would probably suffice.

48 See the following for a list of the livings in this archdeaconry; Borthwick Institute, York, Archdeaconry of the East Riding, Convocation Papers 1685-1857, ER.Conv., Archdeaconry of the East Riding Convocation Poll List, 7 Nov. 1727, St Mary's Beverley.

49 See, L A S Butler (ed.), *The Archdeaconry of Richmond in the Eighteenth Century*, (Yorkshire Archaeological Society Record Series, 146 1990), for information about the livings in this archdeaconry.

50 Baskerville, 'Cheshire Clergy', p. 78, n. 13.

51 HMC, *Portland*, Appendix VI, The Earl of Oxford's Journeys, pp. 98-9, 141.

52 The poverty of the clergy and especially the curates was a widely recognised fact in the eighteenth century. An Act of 1713 gave bishops the right to insist that curates were paid a reasonable stipend of around £20-50 per year. A further Act of 1796 allowed bishops in some dioceses to set a minimum salary of £75 per annum. However the glut of curates undercut each other and by the end of the century the average stipend was around £35. I Collins, *Jane Austen and the clergy* (1994), p. 29.

53 Butler, *The Archdeaconry of Richmond*, pp. 48, 89-90.

54 Leeds City Archives, Temple Newsam MSS., TN PO/10/8/T883, 'Accounts of moneys spent in and about the 1741 election...on Lord Irwin's orders'.

55 P Adman, W A Speck and B White, 'Yorkshire Election Results 1734 and 1742: A Computer Analysis', Appendix to J. F. Quinn, 'Yorkshiremen Go to the Polls', p. 173.

56 BL. Add. 32689, f. 218, John Jenkins to Newcastle, 4 May 1734.

57 Borthwick Institute, York, see Institution Act Books 11, 11A and 12.

58 Both the 1727 and 1742 pollbooks include this information. See also, See Bradford City Archives, Spencer Stanhope MSS., SpSt/11/5/3/20, A list of Mr Fox's Objections.

59 Leeds City Archives, Nostell Priory MSS., NP D3/4/2, 'A List of Objections of Sir Miles Stapylton to Sir Rowland Winn's voters'; Bradford City Archives, Spencer Stanhope MSS, SpSt 11/5/3/12, 'A List of Objections of Sir Rowland Winn to Sir Miles Stapylton's voter's'.

60 S Heywood, *A Digest on the Law* (1790), p. 80; see also J. Simeon, *A Treatise on the Law of Elections* (1790).

61 Heywood, *A Digest on the Law*, pp. 75-6, 77.

62 Hirschberg, 'Government and Church Patronage', p. 113.

63 Baskerville argues that chaplains were more sensitive than most to their patrons needs; see, Baskerville, 'Cheshire Clergy', p. 75.

64 MS. Willis 35, f.2, John Richardson to Browne Willis, 18 Aug. 1722.

65 BL. Add. 32698, f. 325, Viscount Irwin to Newcastle, 16 Nov. 1741; B. L. Add. 32699, f. 103, Irwin to Newcastle, 10 Mar. 1742.

66 Lloyd-Baker-Sharp MSS., D3549 6/1/L5, Sharp to the Duke of Leeds, 19 Jun. 1700.

67 Jackson, *Diary ... de la Pryme*, pp. 54 , 178.

68 Lloyd-Baker-Sharp MSS., D3549 6/1/R16, Sharp to Lady Russell, 4 July 1702.

69 Wentworth Woodhouse Muniments, WWM/I, Archbishop Blackburn to Malton, 3 Nov. 1733.

70 Lloyd-Baker-Sharp MSS., D3549 6/1/N22, the Earl of Nottingham to Sharp, 16 Apr. 1709.

71 D M Owen, 'From the Restoration until 1822', in G E Aylmer and R Cant (eds), *A*

History of York Minster (Oxford, 1979), pp. 241-2.

72 John Le Neve, *Fasti Ecclesiae Anglicanae, 1541-1857*, vol. IV, York Diocese, eds J M Horn, and D M Smith (London, 1975).

73 See above, p. 15.

74 P Smithes (ed.), *The Spectator*, I (London, 1970), no. 112, 9 July 1711, 341; *ibid.*, no. 106, 2 July 1711, p. 325.

75 Borthwick Institute, York, Beverley Minster Papers, Bp. C&P XVII/8, John Midgley to Mr Waller, 9 Nov. 1725.

76 Lloyd-Baker-Sharp MSS., D3549/6/1/29, Sam. Bromfield to Sharp, 19 Mar. 1707.

77 Leeds University, Brotherton Library, Archive of the Dean and Chapter of Ripon: MS. Dep. 1980/1/260.4, Heneage Dering to Mr Hayter, 5 Dec. 1740.

78 This takes party majorities in a particular township to be where sixty per cent of freeholders had polled one way.

79 Cited in Colley, *In Defiance of oligarchy*, p. 154.

80 Wentworth Woodhouse Muniments, MI, Mr Wilton to Malton, 24 Dec. 1733.

81 Not every gentleman would have been noted as such in a pollbook, and similarly this technique for identifying the gentry ignores lesser gentlemen; however, it is relatively useful as a rough guide to the corroboration of gentry and clergy. The gentry were identified as 'Bart', 'Esq', 'Gent', 'Sir'.

82 BL. Add. 24612, f. 14, 'Canvassing notes of a Tory candidates' Agent...'.

83 Borthwick Institute, York, Transmitted Cause Papers, Trans.CP, 1729/3, 1730/2-4.

84 *Ibid.*, Transmitted Cause Papers, Trans.CP, 1709/1.

85 I R Christie, *Wilkes, Wyvill and reform: the parliamentary reform movement in British politics, 1760-1785* (1962), p. 74.

86 *Poll book for 1807* (York, 1807).

87 John Milnes to Fitzwilliam, 17 Jun. 1807 cited in Smith, 'Yorkshire Elections', p. 85.

88 Of the 450 clergy identifiable in both the pollbook and the visitation records, 125 were vicars, 72 rectors, 170 perpetual curates, 61 stipendiary curates with 22 lecturers, school-masters and other office holders.

89 The figures for the whole century are: 1708 – 51 per cent (of the Anglican clergy voted Tory); 1727 – 31 per cent; 1734 – 33 per cent; 1742 – 28 per cent and 1807 – 70 per cent.

90 Ollard, *Herring's Visitation Returns, passim* and Borthwick Institute, York, Visitation book V1806/Exc.Bk; these returns were used to calculate the number of clergy active in the shire.

91 'Fitzwilliam covered by loans, spent nearly £100,000 and Lascelles only a few thousand less; Wilberforce, who prided himself on the support of 'volunteers' against the others' 'regulars', rebuked such extravagance in spending a modest £28,000...', R G Thorne (ed.), *The History of Parliament, 1790-1820*, II (1986), p. 438; see also Smith, 'Yorkshire Elections'.

92 York City Archives, Miscellaneous Election Papers, MSS. M32:9-16, 1784 Canvassing Books. Unfortunately only ten wapentakes appear to have been canvassed and none of these were from the East Riding, whilst only one, Skirack, was from the populous manufacturing districts of the West Riding. However, the results do show a movement away from the Whigs. See also Christie, *Wilkes, Wyvill and reform*, pp. 201-11.

93 P Langford, *Public Life and the Propertied Englishman* (Oxford, 1991), p. 434.

94 W A Speck, *The Birth of Britain: A New Nation, 1700-1710* (Oxford, 1994), p. 191.